THE TRIPLE NET INVESTOR

The Ultimate Beginner's Guide

to Net Lease Properties

DEAN HUNTER

ISBN: 978-1-7905-8378-2

Contents

Overview

SINGLE-TENANT NET-LEASED PROPERTIES ARE SOME of today's most desired commercial real-estate investments. Stable long-term income, high appreciation, and few maintenance requirements have helped make these properties highly prized. The combination of high demand and little inventory has limited the acquisition of these properties to very high-net-worth individuals and investment institutions.

In this book, you will learn about commercial real estate in general and about triple-net properties specifically.

"The Triple-Net Investor; The Ultimate Beginner's Guide to Net Lease Properties"

- Here are some of the topics covered in the book:
- What are the types of NNN properties
- The benefits and risks of investing in NNN properties
- How to find off-market NNN properties
- What are net leases
- What are ground leases
- Commercial-real-estate math

- What is a zero-cash transaction?
- Valuation methods of NNN Properties
- The five biggest mistakes that investors make when purchasing a NNN property
- Everything you need to know about building wealth by conducting a successful 1031 exchange, including:
- What are the requirements of a 1031 exchange
- How to find the ideal NNN 1031 exchange property
- How to use your IRA to invest in NNN properties
- What is crowdfunding and how is it used in commercial real estate
- That is just a small sample of what people will learn in *The Triple-Net Investor.*

Why I wrote this book

Reason One: Commercial-real-estate investing has long been a closed-door good-old-boy network. Unless you have family members or close friends who are active in the commercial-real-estate market, it's just not something you even think about. Most people have never heard of triple-net properties and would not even know where to begin to start learning about investing. Many people remain stuck dealing with burdensome residential and multifamily properties. I am pulling back the curtains and letting the average investor learn about these unique opportunities that we only usually reserve for our private clients at my real-estate company, The Forbes Commercial Group.

Reason Two: I have over a decade of experience in commercial-real-estate investment sales and syndication. Over the course of this period, I have helped hundreds of successful investors purchase hundreds of millions of dollars in income-producing properties.

Reason Three: The NNN market is exploding. Hundreds of properties are being traded in private off-market deals. Properties that are listed on the market are being sold in days and are receiving multiple offers. 1031 exchange buyers, institutional and even foreign investors are buying NNN properties for record high prices.

Reason Four: Commercial real estate is the one area where equity crowdfunding has experienced tremendous success. According to the *Wall Street Journal*, over 500 million dollars has been invested in US commercial real estate through crowdfunding.

Reason Five: I have seen so many property owners pass on incredible opportunities to build generational wealth simply because they lack information about commercial real estate investing. These property owners think they are doing the "smart thing" by holding on to the property. In many cases the property is not producing any significant income. Sometimes the property is producing no income at all. It is so sad to hear these property owners say, "I can just hold onto it for my kids." They would be far better off to sell the property and reinvest the proceeds, tax free, into income producing property of higher value. This book will show them how.

Who This Book is For

This book is for anyone who wants to learn more about investing in commercial real estate in general and single-tenant net-lease properties. This book is ideal for most people, including:

- Investors – who want long-term highly safe investments in trophy properties
- Retirees – looking for safe long-term investments
- Parents – searching for a vehicle to finance the kid's future education
- Real-estate agents – who want to learn about selling and investing in commercial real estate
- Residential investors – who want transition into passive-income-producing properties

- Stock investors – looking to diversify their portfolio
- Employees – looking for alternatives to their 401k

Who This Book is Not For

This book is not for anyone looking for the next get-rich-quick program. This book is a collection of substantive information about investing in commercial real estate.

Chapter 1

Intro to Triple-Net Properties

Triple-net properties are some of the most highly sought-after commercial-real-estate investments in the country. Net-leased properties are appealing to a wide variety of buyers, from high-net-worth individuals to partnerships to large institutional investors like real-estate-investment trusts, life-insurance companies, and pension funds.

Net-leased properties also are very attractive to investors who need to do 1031 tax-deferred exchanges. Net-lease assets give investors a stable safe alternative to the highly unpredictable and volatile stock market. Net-lease properties are often referred to as "a bond wrapped in real estate." Net-lease investments are stable, predictable, and have very little risk.

A single-tenant net-lease property is typically described as a free-standing office, industrial, or retail building that is leased and occupied by one user or one company. Ideally, the tenant has committed to a long-term lease of ten years or more with increasing rent over the lease term. The single-tenant occupier is responsible for paying rent plus some or all the operating expenses of the building, such as taxes, insurance premiums, repairs, and utilities.

There are many benefits to investing in single-tenant net-leased (STNL) properties. STNL properties provide a steady and dependable cash flow because the tenants sign long-term leases. Additionally, the extended nature of the leases makes it very unlikely the property will sit vacant when a tenant does not renew. A property would have to be in a very bad location for a leasing agent not to find a replacement tenant with five years' notice that a lease is expiring.

One of the other major benefits of net-leased properties is the security of the initial investment. For example, when you purchase a net-lease property you will get the payments during the lease term and the added benefit of likely appreciation of the property. In part because of their location and long-term leases, NNN properties are not subjected to the same risk of depreciation as other commercial properties.

Unlike in the stock market where you are subject to continuous fluctuations, you are assured to get the rental payments from your long-term lease, and you are more than likely to see your property appreciate in market value. Net-lease properties allow you to preserve your investment capital.

Net-lease properties are passive investments. A passive investment is one where you get paid and you are not required to do any additional work. In comparison, an active investment requires your time and money. For example, owning an apartment building or even a shopping center requires a lot of work. You must deal with repairs, lease negotiations, rent collections, and other tenant issues. Many owners are transitioning from multifamily to net-lease properties.

Another benefit of net-lease properties is that they can be used to build and pass wealth to future generations. With the assistance of estate planners, an owner can pass on the property and the income associated with it to future generations. Later in the book we will show you how our advisors at the Forbes Commercial Group (www.ForbesCre.com) help owners utilize the benefit of the 1031 exchange to build generational wealth and reinvest gains into new properties that produce even more income.

Chapter 2

WHAT TO LOOK FOR WHEN BUYING A TRIPLE-NET PROPERTY

SINGLE-TENANT TRIPLE-NET PROPERTIES ARE SOME of the most reliable forms of income- producing real-estate ownership. There are four major factors that should be examined when evaluating a NNN property:

1) The location
2) The property
3) The tenant
4) The lease

1) Location, location, location still reigns supreme as the primary consideration in real-estate investing. Is the property in the city or the suburbs? What city is it located in? Is it on a prime corner or a highly trafficked street? The right location includes the concepts of "replaceability" and tenant demand. Often, triple-net investors ignore the importance of location, relying most heavily on the strength of the primary tenant to offset a weaker location. While location risk can be diminished by a strong, national tenant, the better investment choice

includes a strong tenant in a strong location. The cost of the asset often will be higher for the better location, but the ability to replace a tenant in a location that provides greater demand can provide irreplaceable downside protection.

2) The Property: The right property includes the right type and condition of the asset as well as the price paid for the asset. Cost and condition are interdependent in real estate. An asset in poor or fair condition may make a great purchase at a severely discounted price, whereas the best real estate location in the world may make a bad purchase if the buyer pays too much. The major consideration as it relates to the right type of asset is the ability to place new tenants in the space in case a lease is not renewed.

A property uniquely customized to one tenant can be very difficult to fill if the original tenant defaults or does not renew their lease. For example, it is much easier to find a replacement tenant for a building that has housed retail clothing or goods than one that has been built out to serve as a Jiffy Lube.

3) Tenant: Who is a good tenant? The best tenants are national companies with little or no debt and investment-grade credit ratings. When looking for the right tenant, an investor must be careful to distinguish between corporate and franchise-backed leases. There is a big difference between the security provided by a

national corporation when compared to an individual franchisee. The NNN property market is diverse and provides a broad array of tenant options for a client to customize their investment portfolio.

4) Lease: Information pertaining to selecting the right lease is provided in greater detail later in this book. The essential point is that the best leases require a lease term long enough to provide stability, have regularly scheduled rent increases ("lease bumps"), and are free from unfair early termination clauses.

These are the major factors to be considered when searching for an acquisition. There are numerous types of NNN properties that an investor may choose from. The Forbes Commercial Group (www.ForbesCre.com) can help you find the right one for you.

Chapter 3

WHAT ARE THE PRIMARY SINGLE-TENANT PROPERTY CLASSES?

THERE ARE PRIMARILY FOUR MAJOR classifications of single-tenant commercial properties. Retail, office, industrial, and special purpose are the four major categories. These can be further subdivided into subcategories based on the specific characteristics of the tenant. In this chapter, we will examine the various types of single-tenant property classifications, and explore some of the pros and cons to ownership of each type.

Retail single-tenant properties are the most highly prized in the class. However, they can be subdivided by tenants that are fast food providers or restaurants, drugstores and pharmacies, banks, or other retailers.

Fast Food

Fast food restaurants are good single tenants because they tend to be immune from fluctuations in economic conditions. At the Forbes Commercial Group, we advise investors to target well-known, national chains that offer discount and value meals for consumers such as McDonald's, Wendy's, and Chipotle. Fast food restaurants tend to do relatively well in both good and bad economic times. When the economy is not performing well, fast food chains tend to remain stable. Many chains produce discounted menus, and customers tend to eat cheaper and less expensively.

Many consumers go from dining out to grabbing fast food for dinner when finances are tight. When these tenants have long term, leases backed by their parent corporations, the properties they occupy will yield the lowest cap rates. Sometimes fast food tenant leases may be backed by regional or local franchise holders. Quite often, these franchise operators will own several units in a region. While there is an increased credit risk with a regional franchise owner compared to a corporate-backed lease tenant, the risk can be offset with more favorable lease terms.

National chain tenants backed by their corporate parents are in a much stronger barging position. They can demand the best lease terms, such as shorter terms or smaller increases during renewal. Leases backed by regional franchise tenants tend to be longer and have more favorable increase terms.

At the Forbes Commercial Group, we advise investors deciding between franchise and corporate-backed leases that several other factors affect the overall investment decision. First, they should evaluate the location. Secondly, investors should consider the terms of the lease. The overall success of the brand, its market share, and the performance of the store in question are all factors to be considered. McDonald's, Wendy's, Chipotle, Chick-fil-A, KFC, Taco Bell, and Pizza Hut are some of the most highly traded fast food brands. Many investors choose to create a portfolio that includes a variety of retail tenants such as fast food, pharmacies, and discount stores. An examination of these retail tenants reveals additional pros and cons to ownership unique to each. Please contact the Forbes Commercial Group for a more detailed discussion of each.

Necessity-retail providers comprise another popular subcategory of retail NNN properties. Necessity-retail providers primarily include, but are not limited to, drugstores, pharmacies, grocery stores, and smaller convenience stores like 7-Eleven. These NNN properties often provide a good mix of stable corporate- backed tenants and retail products that consumers need, regardless of economic conditions. Consumer necessities such as food and medicine are typically immune from economic velocity.

Many necessity-retail NNN assets are tenanted directly by the parent corporations. Corporate-sponsored leases are even more frequently found in this sort of NNN space than in the alternate classes. Most leases are long term, initially more than 10 years, and these necessity-retail providers have investment-grade credit ratings. Long-term stable leases are common in the necessity-retail NNN space. CVS, Rite Aid, and Walgreens are examples of some of the most popular NNN necessity-retail tenants. Investors should seek leases that include regular lease bumps during the renewal periods or throughout the fixed term of the lease.

Many national chains of grocery stores occupy NNN properties. These are great investments as they typically have A credit ratings. The purchase price of these larger grocery store anchor properties might be too high for individual owners to acquire. This is where the syndication and crowdfunding services of the Forbes Commercial Group can be helpful. Hypothetically, an investor sells a multifamily building for two million dollars. The investor wants to utilize the provisions of Section 1031 of the tax code to acquire a new property and avoid paying capital gains taxes.

A NNN property occupied by Walgreens, Trader Joes, or Giant Supermarket may cost more than six million dollars. At the Forbes Commercial Group, we would team up this investor with similar investors, and by pooling their resources, they could jointly acquire the higher-valued NNN property.

Of course, after selling the multifamily building, the investor could always acquire a smaller convenience store such as a 7-Eleven or even a discount store. Many NNN 7-Elevens have corporate-backed leases. Others may be owned by regional franchisees. At the Forbes Commercial Group, we work with owners to help build a portfolio that includes a variety of NNN retail properties including discount stores.

Discount Stores

Dollar stores and discount retailers are highly sought-after NNN properties. With some leases, landlords participate in a small percentage of sales revenue above a certain base rent. Depending on the success of the store, revenue sharing can provide additional upside to the discount store investor.

Family Dollars and other discount retailers such as Walmart, Marshalls, Kohl's, and other discount retailers share the tendency to perform well in tough economic times. When the economy is struggling consumers tend to buy more discounted or sale items. These discount stores often serve consumer basic needs of food, clothes, and home necessities. Most discount retail locations are corporate-backed leases with initial ten- to twenty-year terms that include multiple renewal options thereafter. Lease bumps average about 3%. Most leases are double-net or triple-net, with minimal landlord responsibilities if any.

Dollar stores provide investors with smaller-footprint standalone locations that are often much less expensive than the discount store locations. Unlike the discount retailers, the major dollar store tenants maintain much lower credit ratings. There are three major companies in the dollar store space: Family Dollar, Dollar Tree, and Dollar General. Dollar Tree just completed a takeover of the Family Dollar brand. Because of the lower credit ratings and the inevitable consolidation and rebranding to take place, these NNN properties trade at a higher cap rate.

Gas Stations

Gas station net-lease properties offer investors the opportunity to purchase well-located assets with nationally recognized brands and product offerings. Gas stations perform relatively well in both good and bad economic conditions.

During an economic downturn, gas consumption may decrease. However, consumer demand tends to maintain spending levels that support the operating costs of the standalone store locations. The convenience retail business of gas stations (the food and beverages) provides additional profit potential. Gas stations come in a wide range of investment-grade-credit tenants. However, individual, and regional franchise owners often back stations.

Gas station leases are typically five to ten years in length with many shorter renewal options thereafter. Investors are always better off buying properties with corporate-backed leases. However, properties backed by individual and regional franchise owners will trade with higher cap rates to offset the additional credit risk.

The national gas station brands with the highest credit ratings include Shell, BP, Texaco, Chevron, and ExxonMobil, among others. While some discount brands such as ARCO and Valero will have lower credit ratings, most major gas stations can provide an investor with a strong long-term tenant with favorable rent increase.

Automotive Repair

Companies that provide vehicle repairs, tune-ups, fluid changes, and parts are common tenants in NNN properties. Unlike many NNN property tenants, businesses that provide automotive repairs or parts are not immune to worsening market conditions.

During less favorable economic periods discount automotive part stores may do well. Customers during these periods will be forced to make repairs on their own that they otherwise would have taken to dealers or independent mechanics. However, as automobiles become increasing technologically advanced, it has become more difficult for consumers to self-repair mechanical or electrical problems.

Automotive-related tenants typically provide leases with terms from ten to twenty years that are NN or NNN in structure. Renewal options of five years or more are common in the original lease. Lease bumps are often 3% per year. The landscape of vehicle repair and parts stores is filled with franchises, so it can be difficult to locate the right type of tenant. As with gas stations, there are also environmental issues to consider at vehicle service facilities.

With both gas stations and other vehicle-related properties, an investor must make sure that the liability for cleanup of any contamination or environmental issues are the sole responsibility of the tenant's parent corporation. AutoZone and Jiffy Lube are the major auto-service-related stores that qualify as high-credit-rated NNN tenants. Both can be great investments with corporate backing.

Telephone & Mail services

Companies that provide business- and communication-related services and products are often a good bet in economically volatile times. Telephone and Internet providers deliver both consumer products and business services whose demand remains relatively stable. National private-sector delivery companies often have strong credit ratings. These companies also provide investors with the possibility of acquiring both retail and distribution locations.

Communication and delivery/carrier tenants usually have long-term leases of ten to twenty years with extended five-year renewal options. Most of the retail locations are in highly desirable high-traffic locations. Most telecommunication leases are NNN and provide modest rent increases throughout the lease term. Most national brand locations are corporate-backed leases. The major telephone providers such as Verizon, Sprint, AT&T, enjoy the highest credit ratings.

FedEx and Kinko's are both owned by the FedEx Corporation and enjoy high credit ratings. UPS offers the highest credit rating of this category of NNN properties. However, many of the UPS locations may be individual franchises.

While FedEx and Kinko's may often have longer lease terms, but they do not always select the most highly trafficked areas.

Casual and Budget Dining

Casual and budget dining restaurants may perform similarly to fast food restaurants. They seek to provide the consumer with inexpensive meals and a cheaper way to "go out." However, casual and budget dining chains vary significantly in their overall performance. Investors must be selective in this asset class, as many chains have struggling parent corporations and, as with fast food, certain locations are better managed by franchise operators than the parent company.

Most leases in this space are fifteen- to twenty-year triple-net leases with renewal options tied to the end of the fixed term. Lease bumps tend to be at least 3% per year. In most major restaurant chains, there are both franchise and corporate-backed locations.

Large corporate parents may own several different brands in this class. For example, Olive Garden, Red Lobster, Longhorn Steakhouses are all owned by Darden Restaurants. Similarly, Brinker International owns Romano's Macaroni Grill, and Chili's. These companies and their various brands have performed relatively well. Companies like Denny's and IHOP have also performed relatively well, but the parent corporations have lower investment-grade credit, and many individual locations are owned and managed by multi-unit franchise owners.

Office

Investment-grade NNN offices include corporate headquarters, distribution facilities, and service locations of large companies with strong, investment-grade credit rating that do not typically operate in retail shopping locations. Examples include healthcare companies, pharmaceutical companies, technology providers, business-to-business services, and consumer-goods manufacturing facilities.

These leases vary but typically include lease terms more than ten years with several predetermined renewal options. Lease bumps tend to be small (1-2% per year) or flat, depending on the importance of the location. "Best in Class": Healthcare providers and pharmaceutical companies with investment-grade credit ratings are often the best tenants to have in NNN real estate. Like food and gasoline, healthcare and pharmaceuticals are ongoing necessities that consumers utilize throughout difficult economic times. Corporate headquarters of major healthcare and pharmaceutical companies are preferred.

If you want the most up-to-date information on the various property classes then give me a call at the Forbes Commercial Group. (Www.ForbesCre.com)

Chapter 4

THE 1031 EXCHANGE – THE GENERATIONAL WEALTH MACHINE

USING SECTION 1031 OF THE U.S. INTERNAL Revenue Code, an investor can sell investment property without paying income taxes. This provision of the tax code is a great wealth builder as it allows an investor to avoid paying capital gains taxes by reinvesting the proceeds (exchanging) from the sale of one investment into another.

1031 exchanges provide an excellent vehicle in which a person can transition from a high maintenance investment into a NNN property. For example, one could transition from a multifamily investment into a NNN asset. Investor A owns an apartment building. The building was purchased ten years ago for one million dollars. While an apartment building might be producing income, it requires constant management. Tired of repairs, slow rent collections, evictions, high management fees, and costly vacancies, Investor A decides to sell the building.

Investor A sells the building for two million dollars. If Investor A reinvests the proceeds from the sale of the apartment building into a new investment property, they do not have to pay any capital gain taxes. There are several mandatory requirements an investor must meet to utilize the 1031 exchange deferment.

1) Use of a Qualified Intermediary

Sellers cannot in any way touch the money in between the sale of their old property and the purchase of their new property. An investor must use an independent third party commonly known as an exchange partner and/or intermediary to handle the change.

The intermediary cannot be someone with whom the taxpayer has had a family relationship or alternatively a business relationship during the preceding two years. The role of the exchange partner/intermediary is to prepare the documents required by the IRS at the time of the sale of the old property and at the time of the purchase of the new property. The intermediary must hold the proceeds of the sale in a separate escrow account until the purchase of the new property is completed. If 1031 documents are prepared incorrectly, the IRS will disallow the exchange.

Example: Andre sets up a special escrow account at his bank for the sale proceeds of his apartment building to go into following closing. He never touches the money and had his bank wire all the proceeds to the title company for his new purchase property. Will this satisfy the qualified intermediary requirement? No. Andre exercised dominion and control over the funds and therefore the exchange will be disqualified.

2) Like-Kind Requirement

To qualify as a 1031 exchange there are several requirements. First, the relinquished property you sell and the replacement property you buy must be of like kind. This is a very broad term under the tax code. Like-kind property is property of the same nature, character, or class. Quality or grade does not matter.

The relinquished property, as well as the replacement property, must be held for investment or utilized in a trade or business. Most real estate will be like kind to other real estate. Vacant land will always qualify for 1031 treatment, whether it is leased or not. Furthermore, commercial property may be used to purchase a rental home or a lot may be sold to buy a condominium.

Section 1031 expressly states that property strictly held for resale does not qualify for an exchange. This means that investors and developers who strictly "flip" properties do not qualify for exchange treatment because their intent is resale rather than holding for an investment.

Both properties must be held for use in a trade or business or for investment. Property used primarily for personal use, like a primary residence or a second home or vacation home, does not qualify for like-kind exchange treatment.

Example 1: Johnny owns a condominium in Miami Beach that he and his wife use as a rental property. He wants to sell it to by an NNN property in Maryland. Does Johnny qualify for the exchange deferment? Yes. The property is used as an investment property and not a personal vacation property.

Example 2: William owns land, which he leases to tenant to operate a gas station. He wants to sell the land and acquire a NNN office building. Would this meet the "like-kind" requirement? Yes.

3) 45-Day Identification Rule:

The Internal Revenue Code requires that the replacement property be identified within forty-five days of the closing of the sale of the relinquished property.

The forty-five days commence the day after closing and are calendar days. If the forty-fifth day falls on a holiday, that day remains the deadline for the identification of the new properties. No extensions are allowed under any circumstances. If you have not entered into a contract by midnight of the forty-fifth a list of properties must be furnished and must be specific.

It must show the property address, the legal description, or other means of specific identification.

A maximum of three potential replacement properties can be identified without regard to price. If you wish to identify more than three potential replacements, the IRS limits the total value of all the replacement properties that you are identifying to be less than double the value of the property that you sold. This is known as the 200% rule. Therefore, more than three properties may be identified as replacements however, if the taxpayer exceeds the 200% limit the whole exchange may be disallowed. Consequently, the logical practice for investors is to keep the list to three or fewer properties.

It is the responsibility of the qualified intermediary to accept the list on behalf of the IRS and document the date it was received. However, no formal filing is required to be made with the IRS.

4) 180 Day Closing Requirement:

The fourth requirement necessary to complete a successful 1031 exchange is that the investor closes on the replacement property within 180 days of the sale of the relinquished property. The property replacement property must be one or more of the properties listed on the forty-five-day identification list. A new property may not be introduced after forty-five days. The 180 days starts from the date of the sale of the relinquished property. The forty-five-day identification period and the 180-purchase requirement run concurrently. When the forty-five-day identification period expires, the taxpayer only has 135 days remaining to close. There are no extensions. Not for title defects, finance contingencies, or otherwise. Closed means title is required to pass before the 180th day.

Example: Kenneth identified a retail NNN property within forty-five days of the sale of his apartment building. The retail property is more expensive and Kenneth requires a bank loan. The bank now informs Kenneth that it will not have completed underwriting to be ready to close within the 180-day period. Can he get an extension? No - Kenneth's exchange will fail.

5) Title Must Be Mirror Image

Section 1031 requires that the title of the relinquished property and the time of the replacement property be mirror image. In other words, the investor listed on the old property be the same investor listed on the new property. If a couple is married and sell the relinquished property than both husband and wife must also be on the title to the replacement property. If a LLC or trust is on title of the relinquished property, that same LLC or trust must be on title to the new property.

If the title of the relinquished property is only in the name of one spouse, but a lender is requiring both spouses to be on title to qualify for financing the replacement property, the husband would have to add the wife to the title of the relinquished property before completing the sale by "quit claiming" his interest to himself and his wife.

Imagine partners in a LLC want to sell their respective interest of a property. To accomplish this objective, the LLC must be liquidated and deeds must be issued to provide the respective partners with a tenants-in-common interest in lieu of a partnership or related interest. Real estate qualifies for 1031 exemption, not partnership interests.

Example 1: David owns a storage facility in his own name. He wants to sell it and buy a NNN retail property in the name of a new limited liability company. Will this transaction meet the requirements of Section 1031? No. The replacement property must be acquired in his own name or he must quit claim his interest to the LLC and himself as tenants in common before the sale of the relinquished property.

6) Must Invest an Equal or Greater Amount

The price of the replacement property must be of equal or greater value than the relinquished property to defer 100% of the tax on the gain. There are two requirements within this rule. First, the new property must be of greater or equal value of the one that is sold. Secondly, all the cash profits must be reinvested.

An investor who elects to do an exchange and take cash out may do so, however, any cash received will be taxed. Taxes must be paid on any funds not reinvested in the replacement property.

An investor may deduct closing expenses and commissions from the sale of the property being sold. If the property is being sold for $100,000,000 and the actual net amount after closing expenses is $950,000. All that is required to be spent for the replacement property is a total of $950,000. Closing expenses associated with the purchase may be added into the purchase, as well as capital improvements completed within 180 days, together with furnishings. A little-known fact is that an investor may make an unlimited number of capital improvements as well as spend up to fifteen percent of the acquisition cost on personal property.

Example 1: Clifford owns a property he paid $1,000,000 for and is now selling for $2,000,000. He has a $250,000.00 mortgage against the property and wants to buy a new property for $1,000,000 with the cash. Does this qualify for tax deferral treatment? No. Clifford is buying down from $2,000,000 to $1,000,000. Accordingly, tax is owed on the amount of the buy down, which is $1,000,000.

Example 2: Paul sells a property for $500,000. He wants to buy a replacement property for $600,000 and obtains a $200,000 loan. Paul uses $400,000.00 of the $500,000 cash that the qualified intermediary is holding. Is his exchange fully deferred? No. Despite buying up, Paul did not use all the cash and will be taxed on $100,000.

Reverse Exchanges

The IRS has set up guidelines that allow an investor to acquire a new property before the first property is sold. This is called a reverse exchange. All previous requirements are applicable...and then some. A reverse may come in handy when a seller does not yet have a buyer for the property that he wishes to sell and is afraid of losing the new property he wishes to acquire.

In this situation, title to the new property is taken in a parking arrangement. The new property is not titled to the investor but instead to the qualified intermediary, who in this situation becomes an "exchange-accommodation titleholder." The old property must be sold and closed within 180 days of first acquiring title to the new property. As soon as the old property is sold the proceeds are then directed to the qualified intermediary, at which time the property may be deeded out of the parking arrangement directly to the taxpayer.

There are a few issues with this type of transaction, in that the investor must pay for the newly acquired property upfront before receiving any funds for the sale of the replacement property. The investor must also be sure that the relinquished property will sell within his 180 days. Reverse exchanges are more likely to be successful when utilizing all cash. Lenders are highly unlikely to finance a property that is titled, even temporarily, to a third party.

It is important that an investor work with a commercial-real-estate advisor who can help identify a replacement property within the forty-five-day period. At the Forbes Commercial Group, we keep an active list of all NNN properties on the market across the country.

The 1031 exchange is an excellent tool to build generational wealth. An investor may keep rolling over the proceeds of selling property to acquire increasingly valuable income producing properties without paying taxes for his entire life. If the investor holds the property until his death, then his heirs will receive a "stepped up' basis to fair market value, and the capital gain is never taxed. The income taxes deferred to the investor now become permanent to his heirs.

The advisors at the Forbes Commercial Group (www. ForbesCre.com) are true experts in 1031 exchanges. Give us a call today for a confidential consultation. We can sell your existing property and help you find a replacement. We work with Co-brokers all over the country, so we know someone in your location.

Chapter 5

NNN Real-Estate-Investment Trusts

A REIT, or real-estate-investment trust, is a company that owns or finances income-producing real estate. Modeled after mutual funds, REITs provide investors of all types with the potential of dependable periodic income streams, diversification, and long-term capital appreciation. REITs typically pay out all their taxable income as dividends to shareholders. In turn, shareholders pay the income taxes on those dividends.

REITs allow anyone to invest in portfolios of large-scale properties the same way they invest in other industries – through the purchase of stock. In the same manner, corporate shareholders benefit by owning stocks. The stockholders of a REIT earn a share of the income produced through real-estate investment – without having to go out and buy or finance property.

REITs are generally divided into two major categories, public REITs, and private REITs. Public REITs are those traded on open exchanges. These are easier to acquire and liquidate. Private REITs are closed funds. This makes them more difficult to acquire shares in. However, these funds are not subject to daily fluctuations in the market as public REITs are.

The two main types of REITs are Equity REITs and Mortgage REITs.

Equity REITs are responsible for the value of the assets. Equity REITs generate income through the collection of rent on, and from sales of, the properties they own for the long-term. Mortgage REITs deal in the investment and ownership of mortgages or mortgage securities tied to commercial and/or residential properties. Their revenue is primarily derived from the interest they earn on mortgage loans.

Today, REITs are tied to almost all aspects of the economy, including apartments, hospitals, hotels, industrial facilities, infrastructure, nursing homes, offices, shopping malls, storage centers, and student housing.

To qualify as a REIT a company must:
- Invest at least 75% of its total assets in real estate
- Derive at least 75% of its gross income from rents from real property, interest on mortgages financing real property, or from sales of real estate
- Pay at least 90% of its taxable income in the form of shareholder dividends each year
- Be an entity that is taxable as a corporation

- Be managed by a board of directors or trustees
- Have a minimum of 100 shareholders
- Have no more than 50% of its shares held by five or fewer individuals

REITs offer investors many potential benefits, including but not limited to:

Liquidity: Stock-exchange-listed REIT shares can be easily bought and sold.

Performance: Over most long-term horizons, stock-exchange-listed REIT returns outperformed the S&P 500, Dow Jones Industrials, and NASDAQ Composite.

Diversification: Over the long term, equity REIT returns have shown little sensitivity to the returns of the broader stock market.

Dividends: Stock-exchange-listed REITs have provided a stable income stream to investors.

Transparency: Stock-exchange-listed REITs operate under the same rules as other public companies for securities regulatory and financial reporting purposes.

Some of the top REITs investing in STNL properties include:
- Realty Income
- NNN
- ARC
- W.P. Carey

- Spirit
- Store Capital
- Agree Realty
- Gramercy Property
- Chambers Street
- Gladstone Commercial

Chapter 6

Ground Leases

What is a Ground Lease?

HAVING A CLEAR UNDERSTANDING OF ground leases is important for anyone with an interest in investing in NNN properties. Unfortunately, this is an area where many investors and inexperienced real-estate professionals miss some good opportunities, simply because they are not well versed in the subject of ground leases.

In this chapter, we'll reveal some insight into how ground leases work, clarify what common ground lease structures resemble, and we'll additionally clear up some regular misconceptions about the ground lease.

As a matter of first importance, what precisely is a ground lease? Ground leases, frequently called land leases, are just a lease of the land area only. Typically, land is rented for a relatively long period of time (50-100 years) to an inhabitant that develops a building on the property. A ground lease distinguishes ownership of the land from ownership of the structures and improvements constructed on the land.

Are Ground Leases a Good Investment?

Although it may appear to be odd at first for a developer or tenant to build on land that is owned by another person, there are many reasons why a ground lease might be a great deal for everyone involved.

Often, the biggest advantage for tenants is that a ground lease provides access to a well-situated land parcel that simply can't be purchased because the owner does not want to sell. In these cases, many big retail tenants widely use ground leases such as Starbucks, Walmart, and McDonald's to build stores at highly desirable locations.

Another advantage of a ground lease is that the tenant does not have to come up with the capital investment necessary to acquire the land in a deal. This significantly lowers the initial equity investment required in a project, freeing up capital for other uses. For the landowner, a ground lease provides a steady income stream, typically from a creditworthy tenant, while still allowing the landlord to keep ownership of the property. Ground leases normally have a reversionary clause, which transfers ownership of the improvements on the land to the landlord at the end of the lease.

For example, Developer X, enters a ground lease for a period of fifty years with the owner of Parcel A. Developer X builds a retail building on Parcel A. Developer X then leases the retail building to CVS Pharmacy for a period of fifty years. At the end of the ground lease period, the owner of Parcel A will have access to the parcel and ownership of the retail building built on the parcel.

For these reasons, ground leases can be a great way to keep property in the family for legacy and wealth-building purposes. The owner receives income from the property while allowing the property to be improved and retains ownership and the benefit of long-term appreciation.

Subordinated vs. Unsubordinated Ground Leases

Ground leases can be subordinated or unsubordinated. A subordinated ground lease is essentially a ground lease where the landowner consents to take a lower position in the order of right of ownership of the land. Essentially, the landowner is pledging the land as collateral for the loan on the improvements, effectively becoming a sub-lender on the project.

Why would a landowner subordinate their interest in a ground lease? There are several reasons why this may benefit the landowner. For example, one benefit would be the facilitation of debt financing to construct a building that will add value to adjacent properties also owned by the same owner of the ground lease. This would provide the landowner with potential long-term financial benefits that far exceed the scope of the initial ground lease. Another possible reason might be that the landowner can negotiate higher lease payments or other more favorable terms.

On the other hand, an unsubordinated ground lease is a ground lease where the landowner maintains its first position in the order of claims on the asset. In this case, a lender would not have the right to take back the land in the case of a default by the tenant. This unsubordinated position is considered much safer for the landowner (superior even to the mortgage), and as such will result in lower lease rates.

Ground-Lease Valuation

Ground-lease valuation is not unlike the valuation of any other lease or cash flow stream. Here we have a clearly defined lease term, a specified lease rate, an escalation schedule, and terminal value. A projection of these cash flows can be created and then discounted to determine a present value.

The value of a ground lease is influenced by subordination, credit quality of the tenant, future attractiveness of the location, quality and value of the improvements, and any other relevant terms of the lease. As with all leases, it's always important to thoroughly read the lease to have a through comprehension of the complete responsibilities of all parties. Ground leases can be complicated. The Forbes Commercial Group advisors are ground lease experts. (www.ForbesCre.com)

Chapter 7

NNN Investor Finance

To SUCCESSFULLY INVEST IN NET-LEASE assets one must have some familiarity with basic commercial-real-estate finance terms. The financing of your net-lease acquisition is perhaps the most important factor in obtaining the maximum return of your investment. In this chapter, we will examine some of the financial terms that you must understand to successfully invest in triple-net assets.

ROI – The formula used to calculate ROI is Net Profits/Investment. Return on investment is the percentage or financial return on the cash invested or initial down payment used to acquire an asset. Return on investment is the benefit to the investor resulting from an investment. A high ROI means that the investment gains compares favorably to investment cost.

NOI – Net operating income - A calculation used to analyze real estate investments that generate income. Net operating income equals all revenue from the property minus all reasonably necessary operating expenses. NOI is a before-tax figure; it also excludes principal and interest payments on loans, capital expenditures, depreciation, and amortization.

Cap Rate – Short for capitalization rate, this is perhaps the most important term in net-lease investing. Essentially cap rate is the net operating income divided by the purchase price. This is the percentage of return on an investor's initial investment. For example, Lee Spurlock purchased a net-lease building for $1,000,000. The building is leased to CVS and the annual rental income is $100,000. The cap rate is therefore 10%. Similarly, if the purchase price remained the same and the rental income is $60,000 per year, then the cap rate would be 6%.

Cap rates on some net-lease assets are as low as 6% (or lower) on some properties and as high as eight percent (or higher). The most significant factor influencing cap rates is demand. The reality of the net-lease space is that there are always more investors looking to purchase properties than there are properties available. It is important to note that with periodic rent increases (rent bumps) over the length of a long-term lease the cap rate will continue to rise because the purchase price remains the same.

The second most significant factor is the commercial tenant. Tenants would like to minimize rental rates. A large national tenant with investment-grade credit is going to be able to get an ideal rate and a long-term favorable lease. For example, CVS is a highly desirable triple-net tenant. A CVS located in a great location with a long-term lease (twenty years with two five-year options) is a great long-term investment, such that a net-lease property in a major market may compel a cap rate as low as 5%. It is like a bond wrapped in real estate. There are usually few such properties on the market at any time. When they do become available, in the one-million to five-million market, they are sold in days and for all cash.

The length of the remaining lease term also significantly affects cap rates. For example, take the same CVS above and change the remaining lease term to four years. It will now be more difficult to sell this building. A potential investor will have to consider the possibility that the tenant will not renew and then they might be stuck with an empty building. This risk will require the investor to receive a higher return on his initial investment. A cap rate in this case could reach 8% or even higher. If this building is in a good location, the reality of this market is that this could be a great buy. The tenant could in fact renew the lease for a long term. Alternatively, a new tenant could also desire the location and enter a long-term lease with even more favorable terms.

Cash on Cash – is the dollar return on the investor's cash down payment. The cash on cash return is net financial return after any mortgage payment on the investment expressed in dollars rather than as a percentage. For example, Jessie Wimbish invests $100,000 to purchase a one-million-dollar building. After mortgage payments, the net rent that she receives is $30,000. The cash-on-cash return is $30,000.

Chapter 8

Zero-Cash-Flow Transactions

Zero Cash Flow – Zero-cash-flow transactions also known as "Zeros," are structured such that all the rent paid by the tenant goes directly to the lender. It is often said that triple-net properties are like bonds wrapped in real estate. Zero-cash-flow transactions are the closest thing to literally being one. These real estate deals are structured like bonds and usually take advantage of high debt to equity ratios (LTV's as high as 85%-90%).

There are several requirements that must be met to complete a true zero-cash-flow transaction. First, the property must be leased to a tenant with investment-grade credit. Secondly, the base lease term must be, at a minimum, twenty years or more. The main advantage of these deals is leverage and depreciation. Zero-cash-flow properties can be attractive for several reasons.

Zero cash flow transactions allow investors to leverage their tenant's investment-grade credit rating, thus allowing them to purchase property with as little as 10% down. These debt structures can be non-recourse and have balloons of up to twenty years. Some are even self-liquidating (the property is owned free and clear at the end of the twenty-year term).

A zero-cash-flow transaction could be a great use of 1031 exchange proceeds. It may even be possible that the down payment on the acquisition of a zero-cash asset could be lower than your tax bill. Zeros are a great way to pass on generational wealth.

Chapter 9

SALE-LEASEBACKS

MOST COMPANIES ARE NOT IN the business of owning real estate. A sale-leaseback enables a company to reduce its investment in land and buildings and free up cash that can be used for more profitable purposes.

A real-estate sale-leaseback is a transaction in which the owner-occupant sells the land and building used in its business operations to an investor and then simultaneously leases the property back from the investor on lease terms agreed to concurrent with the real-estate sale transaction. Sale-leasebacks have become more popular in recent years as an alternative financing mechanism.

In the right set of circumstances, a sale-leaseback transaction can have many benefits to the middle market company that is the real-estate seller.

Lease Terms: Because the seller is also the lessee, the seller has significant bargaining power in negotiating the terms of the lease. In addition to realizing their investment in the real estate, the seller, now the tenant, can negotiate an acceptable lease agreement with the investor acquiring the property. Most sale-leasebacks are structured as triple-net leases. Typically leases run ten to fifteen years. The seller/tenant can also negotiate extension options after the lease expiration, and can also include terms for early lease termination.

Tax Savings: Generally, commercial tenants can write off their total lease payment as an expense for tax purposes. As property owners, the interest expense and depreciation were the only tax deductions available. As a result, a sale-leaseback may have a greater tax advantage.

Real Estate Value: Unlike a mortgage, a sale-leaseback can often be structured to finance up to 100% of the appraised value of the company's land and building. As a result, a sale-leaseback more efficiently uses the company's investment in the real estate asset as a financing tool.

Access to Capital: A sale-leaseback can be used to free up capital that can be used to grow a business through acquisition or investment in facilities, technology, and equipment. Sale-leasebacks can be used as an off-balance-sheet financing structure that gives the seller the opportunity to turn a non-earning asset into growth capital. The sale-leaseback proceeds could also be used for other corporate purchases like the buyout of a shareholder or a special cash distribution to all the shareholders.

Businesses that are struggling with cash flow to pay creditors or are considering a bankruptcy might look to a sale-leaseback for capital. Depending on the value of the company's real estate, a sale-leaseback could provide a significant and fast cash infusion into a company that needs to reorganize.

Sale of a Business: Most private equity groups are not in the business of owning and managing real estate. A prudent business owner who is contemplating selling his company can benefit by taking the real estate out of the company sales transaction and, by doing so, maximize the value of the real estate, and increase the overall gross sale proceeds. If the real estate is left in the transaction, the full value is seldom realized, as the EBITDA multiple often does not value the company's real estate at its true reasonable value.

If you are considering the sale of your company anytime in the immediate future, I recommend you consult with the Forbes Commercial Group concerning a possible lease back. (www.ForbesCre.com)

Chapter 10

CROWDFUNDING COMMERCIAL REAL ESTATE

CROWDFUNDING IS DISRUPTING THE REAL estate industry. Sophisticated commercial-real-estate investments are no longer reserved for institutional money or high-net-worth individuals

In this chapter, we will examine crowdfunding in the context of commercial real estate. First, we will learn the difference between reward and equity crowdfunding. Then we shall examine how crowdfunding is used to invest in commercial real estate.

Crowdfunding has become a major source of new capital for commercial-real-estate deals. It has also become an exciting new opportunity for investors to participate in commercial-real-estate investments that were until recently unavailable to them.

Crowdfunding is defined as the practice of funding a project or venture by raising money from a group of people utilizing the Internet. The JOBS Act of 2012 (Jumpstart Our Business Startups Act) significantly increased the ability to raise money for private real estate investment through crowdfunding. The bill changes major provisions of securities law to allow project sponsors to raise capital from the public utilizing broad-based advertising (general solicitation).

In fact, the industry has generated over $1 billion in real-estate revenue in 2014, and that number is predicted to top $3 billion this year. Projects that have been funded in this way range in value from $100,000 to $25 million, yet most are in the $1-4 million range.

Meanwhile, the U.S. has more than 125 real-estate crowdfunding sites. Less than three years after the JOBS Act made it legal to solicit investments online, real-estate crowdfunding sites are everywhere.

In 2008, Indiegogo and Kickstarter pioneered the reward-based crowdfunding model. They began raising money for new business ventures and products including video games, music albums, books, services, and tech products. Backers of these projects usually received a reward, i.e. an advanced copy of the product, a T-shirt, recognition on the venture's website. Political campaigns, charitable organizations, and some startup ventures relied on this model to raise capital or fund projects.

Real-estate crowdfunding involves multiple investors coming together to pool funds and invest in some real-estate project and share earnings. In fact, it is very like the practice of real-estate syndication. In real-estate syndication, sponsors raise money from multiple investors to finance a real-estate deal or project.

There are two main investment types for investors to choose from. In equity deals, the investors make investments in commercial or residential properties, and in exchange, they hold an equity stake in the property. Each investor shares in a portion of the rental income the property generates. Debt investment involves investing in a mortgage loan associated with a property. As the loan is repaid, the investor receives a share of the interest.

Between the two, equity investments offer the potential for bigger returns, because the return on debt investments is limited to the loan's agreed-upon interest rate. On the other hand, equity investments are riskier and they typically require a longer holding period.

Prior to the passage of the JOBS Act, a syndicator was legally prohibited by securities law from making general solicitations for potential investors. The investment sponsor/syndicator had to have a previously existing relationship with the potential investor before he could offer any investment opportunity. Pursuant to The JOBS Act, the SEC issued new rules to permit general solicitation from accredited investors.

In the United States, to be considered an accredited investor, an individual must have a net worth of at least $1,000,000, excluding the value of one's primary residence, or have income of at least $200,000 each year for the last two years (or $300,000 combined income if married), and have the expectation to make the same amount this year.

Real-estate crowdfunding was first successfully used to provide capital for residential properties. Investors would create limited liability corporations that would provide loans to developers to fix and flip residential properties. As crowdfunding grew in popularity, deals shifted from these small loans to raising equity, mezzanine financing, and debt for larger commercial properties.

Many of the largest crowdfunding websites raise equity capital for real-estate investment sponsors from accredited investors. These crowdfunding platforms primarily deal with real-estate investment sponsors with established track records who have previously syndicated real-estate deals. However, there are others that will host the deals of less-experienced developers.

After vetting, the investment opportunity is listed on the crowdfunding company's website and is marketed through email and the Internet to accredited investors. The crowdfunding company will produce an offering memorandum that provides the details of the offering that contains information such as the location, historical financial and market information, risks, underwriting assumptions, sponsor track records, and exit strategies.

In most commercial-real-estate crowdfunding deals, the sponsors will only use crowdfunding for a small portion of the equity in a project. For example, if the sponsor needs to raise five million to complete a project, he will raise four million from his private network of investors/lenders and raise the remaining one million through a crowdfunding platform. Why Would a Developer Do This? – Because He Is Already Leveraged.

Real-estate crowdfunding platforms structure the investment transactions in one of two ways. Some platforms structure the deals where the individual investors act as a single limited partner. This greatly reduces the burden on the sponsor because he does not have to manage many small individual investors. Other crowdfunding portals simply allow investors to invest directly in the partnership or the LLC that holds title to the company, making them all individual limited partners.

Advantages of Crowdfunding Investing

Transparency: One major upside to using crowdfunding to invest in real estate is the increased transparency for both the investor and developer. Previously, investors might go into a deal knowing very little about the property in question. In terms of monitoring the investment's progress, updates might be infrequent at best.

With crowdfunding, investors enjoy access to multiple online investment opportunities. They have information on availability of multiple investment opportunities. They have at their fingertips, details of the various investment options. They can choose based on type of transaction, deal structure, location, project type, property class, holding periods, fees, and more. Investors can check on their investments online to see how well a project is performing.

Smaller Investment Amounts: Prior to passage of the JOBS Act, sponsors were limited to making offerings to investors with whom they had a pre-existing relationship. Finding these potential investors and explaining the offering is time consuming. At the same time only the most well-connected and wealthiest investors would have access to and opportunity to invest in offerings.

With real-estate crowdfunding, sponsors get offerings out to thousands of potential investors in minutes. This has allowed them to increase the number of people participating in deals and therefore decrease the minimum amounts required to invest in a project. Most real-estate crowdfunding platforms allow investments as low as $5,000.

Lower Fees: Crowdfunding platforms do not have the high overhead costs associated with banks. These costs are often passed down to borrowers in terms of fees. The lower cost of raising money using the Internet allows more money to go directly into the deal. Crowdfunding portals charge significantly lower fees than brokers.

Benefits of Crowdfunding for Sponsors: Developers who need capital to start or complete a project can benefit greatly from crowdfunding. Developers have more flexibility and can raise cash faster. For example, a developer who is highly leveraged and needs additional capital to finish a project might not be able to get a bank loan. Even if he does qualify, he may have to wait months for bank approval. A crowdfunding portal could allow him to raise the needed capital in weeks.

Developers and sponsors also enjoy the benefit of lower costs associated crowdfunding platforms as compared to banks. Crowdfunding platforms also allow sponsors to gain exposure to a mass pool of future investors and clients.

The Top Five Real-Estate Crowdfunding Platforms

FUNDRISE – Founded in 2010 with the expressed goal of "democratizing local investment," Fundrise is one of the oldest and most successful real-estate crowdfunding platforms. The company's first project was the development of an acclaimed D.C. restaurant and retail store. Fundrise has grown since then, but its mission of providing people with a superior way to invest has remained the same.

The portal gives you the ability to invest directly in commercial and residential real estate with as little as $100. It features both public offerings available to non-accredited investors and private offerings available to accredited investors. Fundrise offerings include both equity and debt transactions.

REALTYMOGUL – Founded in 2012, Realty Mogul is another of the most successful online marketplaces for real-estate investing. Realty Mogul connects borrowers and sponsors to capital from accredited and institutional investors. The platform gives borrowers access to debt capital, sponsors access to equity capital, and investors tools to browse investments, do due diligence, and invest online. Realty Mogul offers bridge and permanent loans and joint venture equity. The platform offers both residential and commercial property deals.

REALTYSHARES – Founded in 2013, RealtyShares is a real-estate crowdfunding platform that provides accredited investors access to pre-vetted real estate investment properties and an opportunity to invest as little as $5,000 into each property. The platform offers both residential and commercial investment opportunities.

CROWDSTREET – CrowdStreet is a fundraising platform connecting accredited investors with professionally managed real-estate investments. CrowdStreet features both equity and debt investment opportunities, including multifamily, retail, office, industrial, and land opportunities.

REALCROWD - RealCrowd, which is backed by some of the top venture capitalists in Silicon Valley, aims to connect real estate investors with deals from top real estate companies and developers

Its money-making model is based on "syndication as a service" with fees from real estate developers rather than investors generating its revenue. What this means for investors is that the platform acts as a portal where deals are posted, and you do business directly with the project sponsor. The absence of fees for investors is a big plus. RealCrowd is only open to accredited investors who have a net worth of at least $1 million or income of at least $200,000 a year.

END

Synopsis:

SINGLE-TENANT NET-LEASED PROPERTIES ARE SOME of today's most desired commercial-real-estate investments. Stable long-term income, high appreciation, and few maintenance requirements have helped make these properties highly prized. The combination of high demand and little inventory has limited the acquisition of these properties to very-high-net-worth individuals and investment institutions.

In this book, you will learn about commercial real estate in general, and about triple-net properties specifically.

"The Triple-Net Investor; The Ultimate Guide to Net-Lease Properties"

Here are some of the topics covered in the book:
- What are the types of NNN properties
- The benefits and risks of investing in NNN properties
- How to find off-market NNN properties

- Commercial-real-estate math
- What is a zero-cash transaction
- Valuation methods of NNN Properties
- The five biggest mistakes that investors make when purchasing an NNN property
- Everything you need to know about building wealth by conducting a successful 1031 exchange
- How to sell your apartment building and transition to net-lease properties
- How to use your IRA to invest in NNN properties
- What is crowdfunding, and how is it used in commercial real estate

That is just a small sample of what people will learn in *The Triple-Net Investor*.

Author Bio:

DEAN HUNTER IS A LICENSED real-estate broker and Manager of the Forbes Commercial Group, a commercial real estate firm specializing in investment sales. (ForbesCre.com)

Dean Hunter's experience includes hundreds of investment and leasing transactions. Dean has worked as an associate broker at three of the largest commercial-real-estate companies in the country. Hunter specializes in helping multifamily owners sell while limiting tax liability and transitioning into net-lease properties. Hunter is also the publisher of *Real Estate Agent Magazine* and *CRE Investor Magazine*.

Made in the USA
Las Vegas, NV
23 March 2021

19981746R10036